THE CAIRNGORMS

A pictorial souvenir

NESS PUBLISHING

2 A distant view of the Cairngorms from the north-east

THE CAIRNGORMS

Welcome to the Cairngorms National Park!

The Cairngorms National Park, the largest in Britain, was created in September 2003. This gave official recognition to the uniqueness of the region: Britain's largest area of arctic mountain landscape, including six peaks over 4,000ft/1220m, and one of Europe's biggest nature reserves. It is home to 25% of Britain's endangered birds, animals and plants. But it is far more than just a mountain habitat: moorlands and glens, rivers, lochs and forests all add to the picture, presenting a territory of great scenic beauty, drama and contrast. Here too are the most extensive patches of remnant Caledonian pinewoods. ('Caledonia', Scotland's Latin-Gaelic name, means 'wooded heights'.)

Around the margins of the park and within its boundaries sit numerous towns and villages such as Aviemore, Ballater, Braemar, Grantown-on-Spey, Kingussie and Newtonmore. These settlements provide further variety and interest to the whole kaleidoscope of images and activity that add up to make the Cairngorms a truly special place. 16,000 people live in the National Park whereas approximately 1.4 million people visit the area each year. While this makes tourism the life-blood of the economy, it also represents a major challenge to the ecology of the Cairngorms.

The Cairngorms National Park is big: at 3,800 sq. kilometres it is 40% larger than England's Lake District National Park. Small wonder then that it provides the principal stronghold of several rare birds such as the capercaillie, ptarmigan and Scottish crossbill. The osprey famously re-established itself at Loch Garten in the north of the park and has now spread more widely over Scotland.

One of the few places where you can see the Cairngorms and the sea in the same view. **5**
Pictured from South Sutor, Cromarty, about 40 miles north of the mountains

An abundance of mammals is also present, from the easily observed red deer through the less often seen red squirrel to the elusive pine marten and wild cat. The prospect that any of these *might* be seen adds a frisson of anticipation to an exploration of Cairn Gorm's paths and byways. Other furry faces you might encounter belong to otters and badgers; up aloft, that large wingspan could be a buzzard or a golden eagle.

From a distance, the Cairngorms massif is deceptive to the eye. A casual glance from a train or car window between Kingussie and Aviemore may not be held for long by the smoothly rounded uplift of the hills to the east for, disguised by the sheer scale of the range, they appear more hilly than mountainous. It has to be said, Scotland possesses many mountains that turn the casual glance to a gaze of awe more readily than do these granite mounds at first acquaintance. The Cairngorms make you work to discover their dramatic side as, for the most part, this is hidden from the outside observer. But venture into the glens or climb the mountain paths and the glacier-work is revealed in the scooped corries and the sheer faces of truncated spurs, the near-vertical precipices and buttresses that line the ice-carved valleys. The greatest of these is the Larig Ghru, one feature that *is* visible from afar as a V-shaped gash slicing north to south through the heart of the mountains.

A visit to the Cairngorms leaves one with a host of lasting impressions. With today's heightened awareness of our impact on the world we live in, this is a good place to consider what we stand to lose (or at least damage) if we don't change some of our ways; and also what glories we have the chance to preserve if we do.

The glacial gash of the Larig Ghru carves its way through the Cairngorms. To its left is Ben Macdui, 7 at 1309 metres the highest point in the Cairngorms and the second highest mountain in Scotland

8 A panorama from Creagan Gorm, just north of the main Cairngorms massif. 'Cairngorm' means blue-green hills

10 A corrie in close-up. This is Coire an t-Sneachda, just west of Cairn Gorm itself. Corries were the starting-point of the glaciers which gouged the mountain side, leaving precipices like this

Left: the view from the climb up the corrie wall with the corrie lochan below and Cairn Gorm 11 summit in the distance. Right: looking upwards reveals the rugged nature of the eroding granite

12 By contrast, the easy way up is by the funicular railway. If you let the train take the strain, you will be able to enjoy the vista from the restaurant at the top

Whichever way you reach the tops, terrific views are the reward. **13**
The peak in the distance is Ben Rinnes, about 25 miles to the north-east

14 The Cairn Gorm plateau – a typical summer view, vegetation is sparse and pockets of snow are still in evidence

Small tors and outcrops of granite like this one are a feature of the plateau, **15** especially on the eastern side of the massif

16 A plateau it may be, but a heavily dissected one as this scene shows, with sheer cliffs, lochans and further summits stretching away into the distance

Nowhere is this dissection more dramatic than in Glen Avon with Loch Avon visible far below. **17**
More tors can be seen on the skyline

18 Classic glacial features such as truncated spurs and hanging valleys are clear to see in this winter view of Loch Avon. At more than 750m above sea level it is one of Scotland's highest lochs

A summer storm brews above the north-west corries. 19
Cairngorms weather is notorious for its habit of deteriorating with alarming suddenness...

20 ...but some days it treats walkers to unbroken sunshine.
Heather in full bloom and a lonesome pine grace the slopes of Meall a Bhuachaille (810m)

From the summit of Meall a Bhuachaille are views like this, **21**
a patchwork of lochans and remnants of ancient Caledonian pine forest

22 Left: capercaillie. This magnificent large grouse is down to around 1,000 breeding pairs.
Right: ptarmigan, seen here in its winter plumage. They generally keep to the higher mountain areas

Left: red squirrels remain plentiful for now at least, but may require patience to see them.
Right: red deer are, if anything, too plentiful, but what a fine sight!

24 The north face of the Cairngorms massif resplendent in the first snows of winter

26 Left: it's a long way down from Cairn Gorm (1244m) to Glen More where the reindeer herd is based. Right: reindeer have roamed the hills above the glen since 1952

Loch Morlich, seen here on a still summer morning, is in Glen More. **27**
With sandy beaches at various points on its shore it's an idyllic spot to while away a day like this

28 Loch Morlich showing that it can be equally calm in winter

Looking in the opposite direction, the sun sinks below the surrounding hills

30 Two minutes before this photograph was taken all was shrouded in mist... as it clears, the Larig Ghru comes into sight, plunging down beside the path to Ben Macdui

Five minutes later and it's sunlit uplands all the way. **31**
This is the northern end of the Larig Ghru with Aviemore just visible in the distance

32 From near the summit of Ben Macdui: the southern end of Larig Ghru cradles the infant River Dee

Beneath a typical Cairngorms summer sky with its mountain-generated clouds, **33**
the Dee turns towards the eastern edge of the Cairngorms. See also pp77 & 78

34 Although the plateau has many fairly level areas the boulder fields can be difficult to walk on and tricky to navigate in mist. In this terrain the path is a line of cairns

Across the Larig Ghru from the slopes of Ben Macdui are the twin peaks of **35**
Cairn Toul (left, 1291m) and The Angel's Peak (1258m)

36 As with most of the Cairngorms mountains, Cairn Toul looks like a fairly gentle summit from a distance but shows a very different character in close-up

The Angel's Peak is even more dramatic. Lochan Uaine can just be seen in the bottom of the corrie **37** ('corrie' – or 'coire' in its Gaelic spelling – means cauldron)

38 A little further north along the same ridge is Braeriach (1296m) which demonstrates very well
    why the name 'cauldron' was given to these glacial features

This close-up of Braeriach shows clearly the contrast between the plateau and the plunge. 39
Potential danger for the unwary walker, playground for the experienced climber

40 On its opposite side, the eastern slopes of Braeriach run down to Glen Einich within which lies the beautiful Loch Einich

Glen Einich runs north to the Rothiemurchus Forest where another watery gem, **41**
Loch an Eilein, hides amongst the wooded hills

42 East of the mountains lies Badenoch & Strathspey, location of settlements such as Kingussie. The name is derived from the Gaelic meaning 'the head of the pinewood'

Ruthven Barracks, just outside Kingussie, is one of four defensible barracks built to police the **43** Highlands after the 1715 Jacobite uprisings. It was completed in 1721

44 Just north of Kingussie, Newtonmore is home to the Highland Folk Museum which brings to life the domestic and working conditions of earlier Highland peoples

It encapsulates human endeavour and development in Highland life from the 1700s to 45
the present day through activities and re-enactments like those shown above

46 Autumn colours in the birch and pine slopes of Craigellachie Nature Reserve on the western edge of the town of Aviemore

The sound of the bagpipes and drums comes to the centre of Aviemore as part of a civic event **47**

48 The osprey became extinct in Scotland in 1899 but re-established itself here at Loch Garten in 1959. Today an RSPB observation centre enables visitors to watch them

The River Spey at Boat of Garten, so named because the river used to be crossed by ferry here **49**

50 The Strathspey Railway runs steam and other heritage trains between Aviemore and Broomhill. On the way the trains stop here at Boat of Garten

At Carrbridge the River Dulnain (a tributary of the Spey) flows under the remains of **51** the old packhorse bridge built in 1717

52 East from Carrbridge is Grantown-on-Spey, a fine example of a Georgian planned town – one of the first to be set out in this fashion, in the 1760s

It has many historic buildings, a tree-lined Square and striking Georgian and 53
Victorian architecture as well as this attractive park

54 A delightfully traditional shop front in Grantown reflects the many outdoor pursuits to be enjoyed in the vicinity

Journeying south-east from Grantown around the eastern edge of the Cairngorms presents 55
this view of Strath Avon (the river first seen on p.17 flowing out of the loch)

56 The Cairngorms northern escarpment at sunset

58 Continuing a clockwise circuit of the Cairngorms bring us to the high-set village of Tomintoul. The elegant statue on the right is set above the drinking fountain

A farmhouse reconstruction in Tomintoul's museum, which is part of the tourist information centre **59**

60 Corgarff Castle, a few miles on from Tomintoul, stands bright and lonely in upper Strath Don. Dating back to the 15th century, this fine tower house has an inevitably turbulent history

After several burnings, it was re-fortified after the 1745 rebellion with the addition **61**
of the star-shaped outer wall, designed to aid defence by musket

62 At the south-easterly corner of this tour lies bonny Ballater. Its origins go back to the 13th century, but it was from 1770 that a planned town came into being

The purpose of this development was to exploit the healing waters of a nearby spring. **63**
Healing of another kind is dispensed from today's church, seen here along with the war memorial .

64 Ballater grew again following the arrival of the railway from Aberdeen in 1866. Although the line was closed in 1966 the Old Royal Station remains active as an information centre and museum

The station was used by Queen Victoria on her way to and from Balmoral. **65**
This tableau in the station building re-creates her final departure from Ballater

66 South-west of Ballater is an outlier of the Cairngorms range, with the confusingly named mountain of Lochnagar (1154m) at its centre. Pictured here from Glen Muick

Loch Muick lies at the head of the glen. The largest loch in the Cairngorms, on a clear day **67** its waters are almost unrealistically blue. Lochnagar rises in the background

68 Once persecuted right back into the far north-western Highlands, the pine marten has re-established itself more widely and once again inhabits the Cairngorms

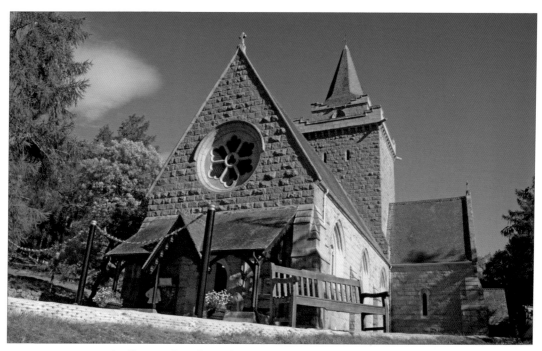

West of Ballater is the village of Crathie, whose church (above, opened 1895) has been **69** made famous by royal patronage due to its proximity to Balmoral Castle

Balmoral has been a royal castle for 160 years, Queen Victoria and Prince Albert having signed the lease in February 1848. They soon began negotiations to buy and in June 1852 Prince Albert concluded the purchase. By now the building they had leased was deemed inadequate and plans were drawn up for a larger castle. Queen Victoria herself laid the foundation stone in 1853 and the new castle reached completion in 1856. The original building, which they had continued to occupy in the meantime, was then demolished.

The castle is open to visitors from April to July and offers much of interest. The Ballroom houses many items which are normally on display within the castle. The walls are decorated with paintings by Landseer and Carl Haag. In the display cabinets are silver statues together with precious porcelain. There are further exhibitions in the Carriage Hall Courtyard describing the history and natural environment of Balmoral and which look at the work of the different Estate Departments. The gardens, which were started under the supervision of Prince Albert, have been expanded and improved by successive members of the Royal Family.

Balmoral Castle in autumn

72 Royal Lochnagar distillery was granted a Royal Warrant of Appointment by Queen Victoria in 1848. It is set in beautiful scenery close to Balmoral Castle. Visitors can tour the premises

Heather is one of the defining plants of the Highlands. This heather garden at 73
Royal Lochnagar distillery contains many varieties

74 Continuing westwards on the last leg of this tour brings us to the village of Braemar.
It is the highest and most mountainous parish in the UK and hosts the annual Braemar Gathering

Alongside the War Memorial, an aero-engine from a plane that crashed nearby **75**
in the Second World War is on display

76 John Erskine, Earl of Mar (1558-1634) started building Braemar Castle in 1628.
Currently undergoing restoration, it will re-open to the public on 15th May 2008

The River Dee meanders through pine forest west of Braemar, its character now
considerably different from that in the picture on p.32

78 A couple of miles further upstream is the Linn ('gorge pool') of Dee.
The spectators on the left are looking out for leaping salmon

With the sun about to say goodnight to the distant summit of Cairn Gorm, **79**
it's time, briefly, for the clouds to take centre stage

Published 2008 by Ness Publishing, 47 Academy Street, Elgin, Moray, IV30 1LR
Phone/fax 01343 549663 www.nesspublishing.co.uk

All photographs © Colin and Eithne Nutt except pp.7 & 18 © Scotavia Images; pp.22 (both) & 48 (inset)
© Mark Hicken; pp.23 (both) & 68 © Charlie Phillips; p.26 (right) © Cairngorm Reindeer Herd;
p.40 © Jimmy Mitchell; pp.44 & 45 © Highland Folk Museum; pp.70 & 71 © Balmoral Estates

ISBN 978-1-906549-01-5

Front cover: Loch Morlich and Cairngorm; p.1: Cairngorms National Park roadside sign; p.4: Coat of Arms in Fife Arms Hotel, Braemar;
this page: ducks on Loch Morlich; back cover: the Royal Bridge, Ballater